I have deliberately not included a CD with this book because I strongly believe that musical development is a personal journey.

I do not want you to merely copy my interpretation but to create your own.

Most of the music that follows was written by me. I will be highly delighted if you create an interpretation that pleases you so much that you keep it in your repertoire.

www.guitarmaestro.im

Play Guitar

Play Guitar

John Snowdon

Matador
9 Priory Business Park
Kibworth Beauchamp
Leicestershire LE8 0RX, UK
Tel: (+44) 116 279 2299
Fax: (+44) 116 279 2277
Email: books@troubador.co.uk
Web: www.troubador.co.uk/matador

ISBN 978 1783065 042

British Library Cataloguing in Publication Data.
A catalogue record for this book is available from the British Library.

Typeset in Bembo by Troubador Publishing Ltd

Matador is an imprint of Troubador Publishing Ltd

The way to practice

1. Identify a problem.

2. Isolate it.

3. Apply or invent an exercise to overcome it.

4. Work at it.

5. Replace it in its context.

6. Move on to the next problem.

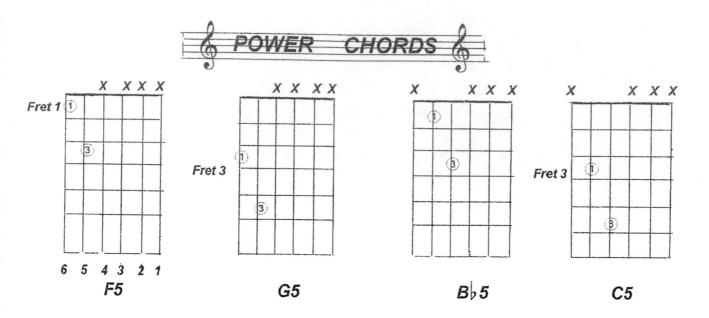

POWER CHORDS

F5 **G5** **B♭5** **C5**

Do not play the strings marked with an X.

This exercise is designed to get you started and used to playing your guitar.

These "shapes" are not really chord shapes but do produce an interesting sound.

Pluck these strings with thumb and first finger four times each before moving to the next shape.

This is where notes appear on the Treble Cleff (musical score).

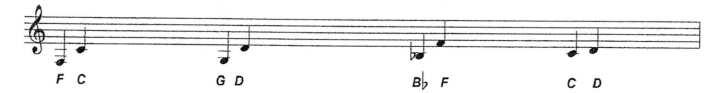

F C   G D   B♭ F   C D

Play around with these shapes until you feel a little more used to holding and playing your guitar and then go to the next stage – True Chord patterns. See page ten.

Introduction

In this tutor I have endeavoured to give the beginner an introduction to making music with the guitar which is easy to comprehend.

There are many ways in which the guitar can be played: as a solo instrument, or as an accompaniment to a song. It is hoped that this tutor will enable the accomplishment of both aims.

I have included a small amount of musical theory in the belief that a knowledge of the "grammar" of musical construction will give the player a wider understanding and thereby a greater enjoyment of music; more satisfying than the mere playing of chord progressions.

Chord progressions are, however, used to encourage various facets of technique.

Music making is a natural talent and can bring piece of mind and enjoyment not only to the player but also to the listener and I do hope that the beginner will find such pleasure and satisfaction through the study of this tutor.

Perseverance is the secret of success, so work at it but please do remember the prime object is to have **FUN.**

AND NOW TO WORK.

Guitar Fretboard

Your guitar consists of six strings placed on a fretboard, numbered one to six. The highest sounding string being the first and the lowest the sixth.

Pluck each string and listen to the sound they produce starting with the first (the highest) down to the sixth (the lowest).

Each of these sounds is known as a musical note and because you are plucking the strings without the use of your left hand you are playing the strings in the **OPEN POSITION**.

The small wires crossing the "**FRETBOARD**" are known as **FRET WIRES** and each space between these wires is known as a **FRET**.

Study the illustration of the guitar fretboard on the next page.

You will see that each string is given a letter to identify it. Learn the name of all six strings.

We will consider written music a little later but for the moment look at the music stave illustrated below the fretboard and note the position of the notes found on the open strings of your guitar.

Don't worry if you cannot understand music notation at the moment. All will be explained later.

Guitar Fretboard

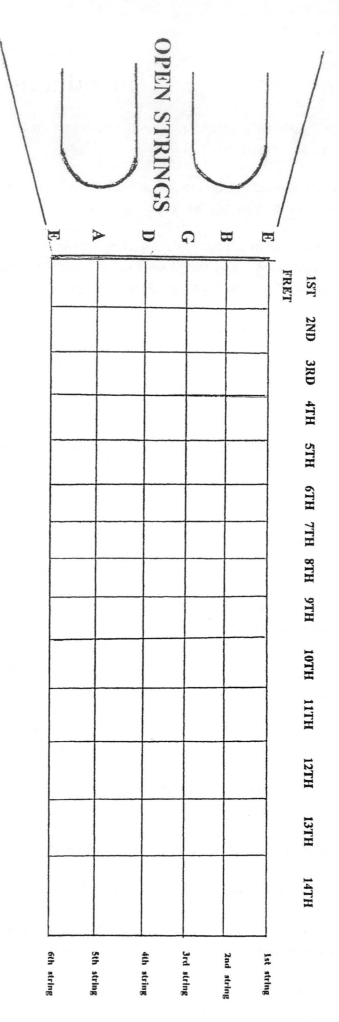

Holding the guitar

The right hand is used to pluck the strings and the left hand is used to hold down the strings on the fretboard.

Classical position

This is by far the best position as it enables the greatest amount of support for the instrument.

Sit on the front edge of your chair, supporting your left foot on a footstool. Place the guitar on your left thigh with the back resting on your tummy.

Place the right arm on top of the guitar so that it pivots and allows the right hand to hang naturally, approximately three centimetres above the strings. Do not let the wrist touch the guitar.

Position your left hand on the neck of the guitar with the thumb on the back. Do not let the thumb creep over the top of the fretboard as this will restrict the movement of the fingers.

You may wish to have your guitar on your right thigh, if you do make sure your left hand palm does not touch the neck of the guitar and that your left shoulder does not dip towards the floor.

Tuning the guitar

If you have access to a piano then you can use the following diagram.

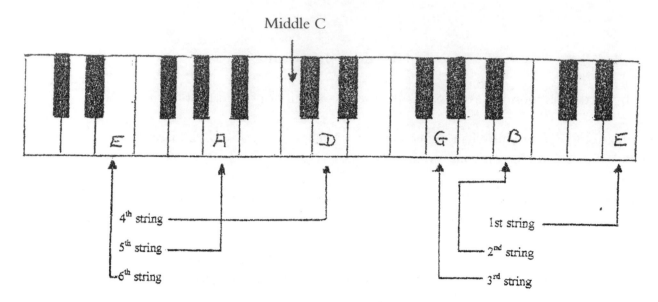

Middle C

4th string
5th string
6th string
1st string
2nd string
3rd string

As an alternative you can use a pitch pipe which incorporates six separate pipes, each one representing the note found on a particular string.

An alternative to the above is a tuning fork. Although it is possible to obtain a tuning fork that is tuned to "E" – the note found on the first open string – most music shops stock those tuned to "A".
To use an "A" tuning fork hold down the first string on the fifth fret i.e. –

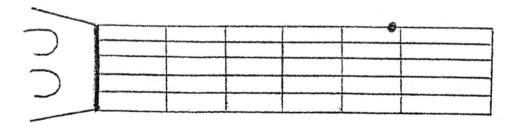

To use the tuning fork tap it on your knee and then place it on the bridge of your guitar. NOT THE BODY OR FRONT SOUND BOARD! As this can cause damage.

This will give you the pitch of the note (A) to which you should tune the first string, adjusting the string tension by means of the tension nut.

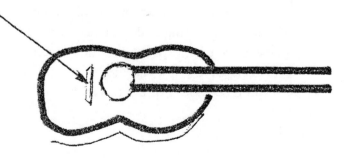

It is now possible to purchase electronic tuning devices of which there are several designs, all of which give accurate readings. Your local music shop will be able to advise you.

The most important task at this point in time is to tune the strings in relation to each other. Providing this is done a small error in pitch is not serious unless you intend to accompany or play with other musicians when you will need to be more accurate.

Assuming that the first string is reasonably in tune the other five strings can be tuned in the following manner:

Second String (B) Hold down this string at the fifth fret and pluck it, adjusting the string tension until the note produced sounds the same as the first string played open (E).

Third String (G) Hold down this string at the fourth fret and pluck it, adjusting the string tension until the note played matches the sound on the second string played open.

Fourth String (D) Hold down this string at the fifth fret and pluck it adjusting the string tension until the note produced matches that found on the third string played open.

Fifth String (A) Hold down this string at the fifth fret and pluck it, adjusting the string tension until the note produced matches that found on the fourth string played open.

Sixth String (E) Hold down the string at the fifth fret and pluck it, adjusting the string tension until the note played matches that found on the fifth string played open.

As you progress with your guitar you will learn pieces incorporating notes found by holding down the strings higher up the fretboard, but for now we will be concentrating on the first five frets in what is known as the **FIRST POSITION**.

When the first finger of the left hand is placed on a string at the first fret we are playing in the **FIRST POSITION**.

When we play with our first finger at the second fret we are playing in the **SECOND POSITION**. And so it goes all the way up the fretboard.

Fingers of the right hand are usually indicated by the names:

Pulgar – (p). Indigo – (i). Medio – (m). Anular – (a).

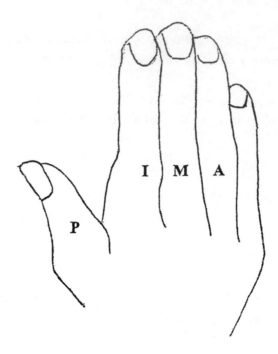

Only the initial letters are used as indicators in music :-

p – Thumb
i – Index finger
m – Middle finger
a – Ring finger

Pease note that the little finger is not used. On occasions you will find the right hand fingers indicated by a series of dots and crosses i.e.

P	I	M	A			P	I	M	A
X	.	..	...	OR		x	.	.	.
								.	.

There are two basic ways of plucking the strings with the fingers on the right hand:-

TIRANDO   –   FREE STROKE
APOYANDO –   REST STROKE

The **REST STROKE** is of most importance when there is a melody note to be played and is always used to accentuate the melody.

The rest stroke is effected by plucking the string with the nail and allowing the pad of the finger to "rest" on the next string.

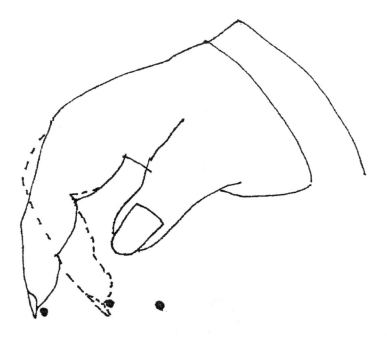

Free Stroke

This is played with the desired string plucked as before but finishing the movement above the next string.

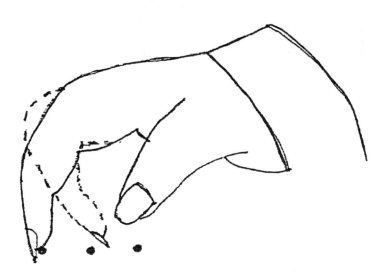

Exercise

Using rest stroke (Apoyondo) and using the right hand fingers **i and m** alternately, pluck the first string (E) four imes, then the second string and so progress up all six strings.

Repeat the same exercise using m (Medio) and a (Anular).

Repeat the same exercise using I (Indico) and A (Anular).

Note – Always keep the thumb in line with the sixth string.

Left Hand

Thumb – Always keep the thumb behind the fretboard and never allow it to creep over towards the sixth string.

The left hand fingers are numbered·

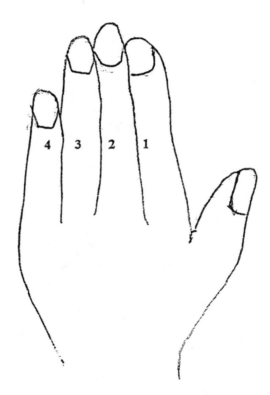

Exercise

Place the left hand fingers upon the fretboard as follows:

First finger (1) on the first string (Top E) at the first fret. Pluck the string with i using a rest stroke.

Follow this with the second left hand finger (2) at the second fret, playing a rest stroke with m.

Always use the tips of the left hand fingers in order to avoid touching the adjacent strings.

Based on the left hand fingering, complete the exercise as per the following fingering to coincide with the numbers of the frets:

      1.2.3.4.   4.3.2.1.   1.4.3.4.   2.4.3.4.

Play the exercise with the alternative fingers m.a. and i.a.

Having mastered the exercise in the first position (first fret) continue up the fretboard from second position (second fret) and so on up to the fifth position (fifth fret).

Repeat the exercise on all the other strings.

Practice slowly: SPEED WILL ONLY COME WITH DELIGENT PRACTICE.

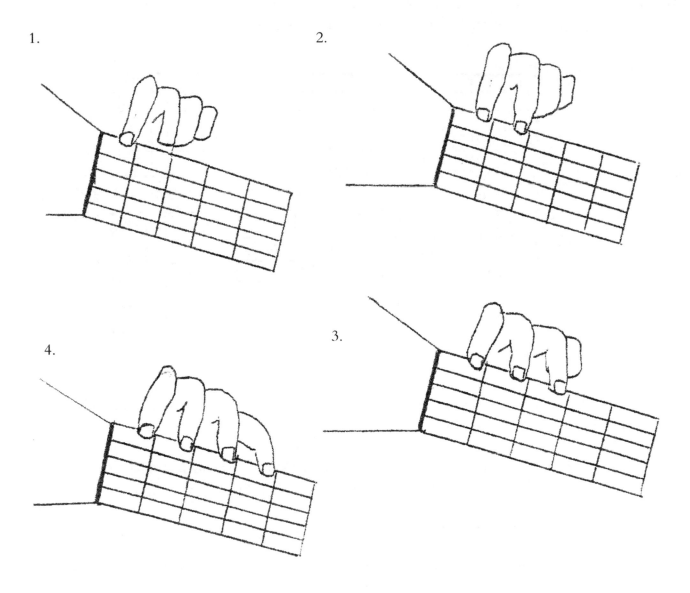

1.

2.

3.

4.

One of the quickest ways to produce results on the guitar is to strum the strings with a downward movement of the right hand thumb (P) whilst holding down **CHORD SHAPES** with the left hand fingers.

There is a tendency to press the strings down with a lot of unnecessary pressure.
Place your first finger lightly on the first string, first fret and pluck the string, slowly increasing the pressure until a clear note is heard. You will be amazed at how little strength is needed.

Here are some of the chords used in popular songs. The circled numbers in the **CHORD BOXES** represent the fingers used to hold down the strings.

e.g. To play the chord of C major: Place the first left hand finger on the second string, first fret.
Place the second finger on the fourth string, second fret.
Place the third finger on the fifth string, third fret.
Do not play the sixth string marked x

Try to keep the left hand fingers on their tips and keep the knuckles parallel to the fretboard. In other words do not let the fingers lean towards the left.

Strum the chords four times each. Concentrate on effecting a smooth progression between chord shapes and remember to PRACTICE SLOWLY. Be sure that all strings produce a clean note.

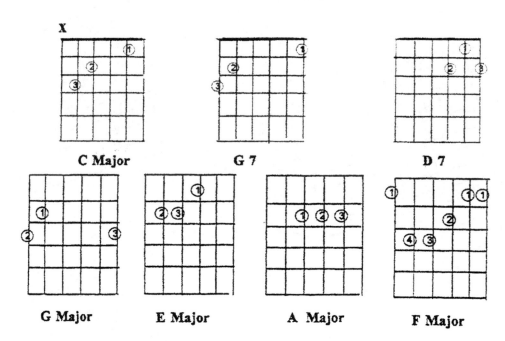

The barre chord F major is initially quite difficult to execute and care must be taken in order to avoid creating too much strain in the left hand.

Try to master this chord shape in the fifth position (fifth fret). Do not press the first finger too hard on the strings as this will cause the middle knuckle to raise away from the strings.

There will be more detailed study of barre chords later in the tutor.

Instead of strumming the strings, now practise the above chords by plucking the strings individually as follows:

Use the thumb (p) to pluck the sixth and fifth strings and i-m-a to pluck the third, second and first strings in these patterns: P.I.M.A.   P.I.M.A.I   P.I.A.I.M

EXERCISE TO STRETCH LEFT HAND FINGERS.

1. Place the first finger on the left hand on the sixth string, first fret (the note F) and leave it there until the exercise is completed.

2. Place finger number four on G sharp. Sixth string, fourth fret.

3. Sound the string with i finger of right hand using a rest stroke.

4. Lift the finger and play the same string open with m of right hand.

5. Place finger number four on C sharp. Fifth string, fourth fret keeping the first finger on F.

6. Pluck the string with I finger of right hand using a rest stroke.

7. Now play the same string open.

8. Repeat on other strings with first finger remaining on F at the first fret.

9. Now repeat with the remaining strings.

10. Reverse the exercise by holding down the G sharp fourth fret, sixth string and play across the first fret with the left hand finger number one. Second fret with finger number two e.t.c.

At the first sign of strain relax and do something else. It is important not to overtax your muscles.

Now practice the following two chords until a smooth progression is obtained from one to another. Use strings five, three, two and one for this exercise.

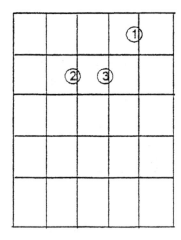

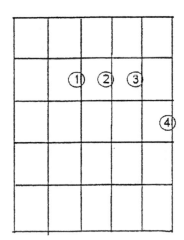

A minor   A 7

Written Music

Music is written on what is known as the **STAVE**, **STAFF** or **CLEF** and consists of five lines and four spaces.

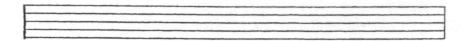

At the beginning of a piece of music you will see an elaborate letter G. This signifies the Treble Clef.

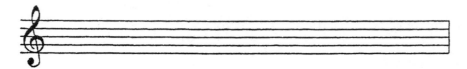

Notes are placed on the Treble Clef, each of which represent a particular sound.

Pluck the strings of your guitar individually and listen to the different sounds. All are different and that difference is known as the "pitch" of the note.

Notice that there are several notes represented by the same letter. They sound quite different however – like the two Es found on the first and sixth strings of your guitar played open.

The notes shown above are found on your guitar in the following positions:-

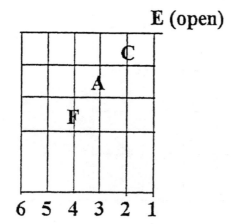

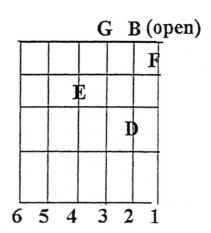

It is now time to look at the different notes that make up a piece of music.

NOTES

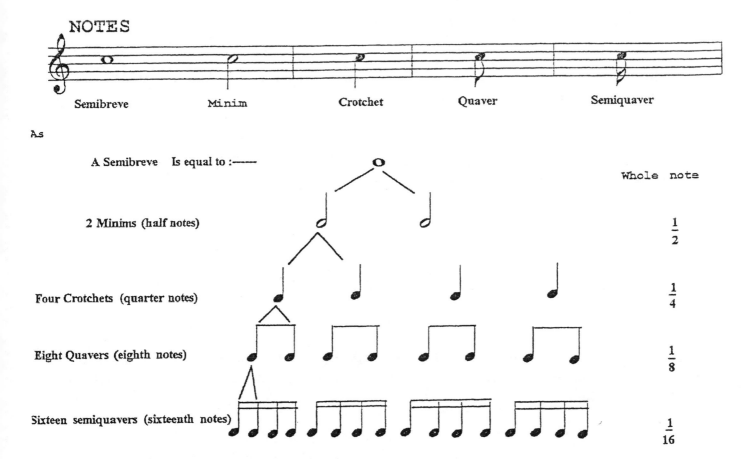

As well as giving us the pitch of a particular sound, the different types of notes as illustrated above tell us how a particular note should last in audible time. That is the length of time a note should last relative to the other notes in the music.

To explain the relationship between notes in a somewhat easier way, imagine that a semibreve is sixteen centimetres long in audible time. Therefore:

A minim would be eight centimetres long.
A crotchet would be four centimetres long.
A quaver would be eight centimetres long.
And a semiquaver would be sixteen centimetres long.

RESTS

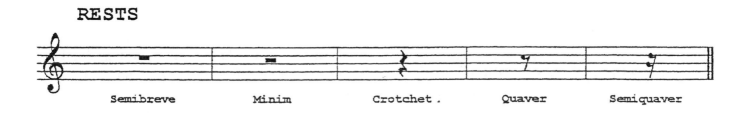

We will discuss the function of rests at a later stage. For now we will concern ourselves with musical notes and their relative values and pitch.

When we listen to music we become aware that it is divided into strong and not so strong beats, hence we are aware of waltz time, for instance, where it seems natural to count in threes.

Music is usually split up into groups of three or four beats with the accent falling on the first beat of the group.

The number of beats between the strong beats divide the music up into sections known as **BARS** with the first (accented beat) acting as the first beat of the bar.

BAR LINES

Music is written on what is known as the **STAVE, STAFF** or **CLEF** (they mean the same thing). This consists of five lines and four spaces and, as we have already seen, each of these lines and spaces relate to a particular pitched note.

At the beginning of each stave we have a clef sign. For some instruments and voices it is necessary to utilise two such signs – a base clef and a treble clef. We, however, need only one of them. The Treble Clef.

The next thing we notice is that we have some sort of fraction to deal with e.g. $^3/_4$ and $^4/_4$.

These fractions in fact give us instructions with regard to the number of beats in a bar and the type of beat. $^3/_4$ for instance tells us that there are three beats in the bar. In bar two of the examples above you will see minims which, as a minim is equal to two crotchets, accounts for two of the three beats in the first example and two of the four beats in the second.

So – the top figure tells us the number of beats in a bar.

The bottom number (on our examples, 4) tells us the type of note that makes up the bar. In our examples quarter notes or crotchets.

Look closely at the two examples and tap out the value of the notes on your knee whilst counting aloud the number of beats in the bar. In bar three of the first example in order to give the correct value to the two quaver notes, count the whole bar **one and two and three and.**

e.g.

(one and)   (two and)   (three and)

Work on similar lines with both the above exercises and when you have mastered them play them on your guitar. Refer to the fretboard diagram at the beginning of the book to check the names of the notes and where they are to be found on the guitar.

REMEMBER TO USE REST STROKES

Exercises on open strings.

Use rest strokes and the right hand fingering shown.

EXERCISE A

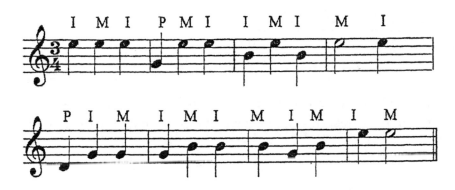

EXERCISE B

KEY SIGNATURES

In order to maintain the correct distance between notes in a scale we have to introduce **SHARPS** and **FLATS**. We can illustrate this point by considering the scales of C major and G major.

As we can see from the above, the scale of C Major does not need sharps or flats because the semitones (E to F and B to C) occur in the correct positions.

If, however, we start the scale on any other note the sequence of tones and semitones is altered.

In this example we still have the first semitone in the correct position (between B and C) but the second one is in the wrong position (between E and F). To correct this anomaly we must introduce a sharp and the note to be sharpened in this example is F.

We have now put the semitone in its correct position – between F sharp and G (Tee-Doh).

Rather than use individual accidentals (sharps, flats and naturals) for individual notes, it is neater to put them at the beginning of the clef. This means therefore that the scale of G Major is written thus:

A more detailed explanation is given on the next page.

Remember that when sharps or flats occur in the **KEY SIGNATURE** they influence the pitch of those notes throughout the piece of music. When they are introduced to individual notes within a piece they only last until the end of the bar in which they occur.

To restore a note to its original pitch within the bar requires a reinstatement by means of a sharp, natural or flat sign.

SHARPS ♯ FLATS ♭ and NATURALS ♮ are grouped together under the heading ACCIDENTALS and alter a given note by raising it or lowering it by one semitone (or half tone).

This is one fret on the guitar.

A SHARP RAISES A NOTE BY ONE SEMITONE

A FLAT LOWERS A NOTE BY ONE SEMITONE

A NATURAL RETURNS A NOTE TO ITS FORMER PITCH

Musical notes take their names from the alphabet: A, B, C, D, E, F and G. Only these seven letters are used. A scale may begin on any of these letters.

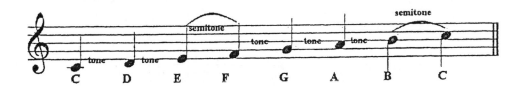

There is only one semitone between B and C.
There is only one semitone between E and F.

In the C major scale above, the semitones fall in the correct places (between B and C and E and F) so there is no need to introduce accidentals.
If however we start on G the second semitone falls in the wrong place.

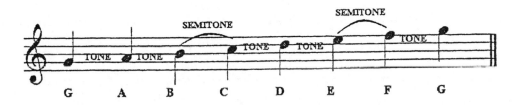

The first semitone is in the correct place but the second one is between the fifth and sixth notes (MEASURES).
Play these notes on your guitar and notice they do not sound correct.
To overcome this problem we have to sharpen the seventh note thus:

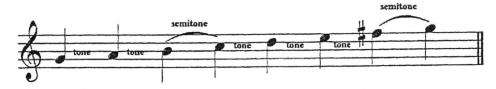

Now the semitones are in the right place and the scale sounds correct.
It would be cumbersome to put a sharp (accidental) against every F so we put it at the beginning of the music.

Now every F will be sharpened no matter what pitch i.e. high or low.

MAJOR KEYS

The tonic of the key (first note in the scale) is always a semitone above the last sharp in the key signature.

The tonic of the key is always two and a half tones below the last flat in the key signature.

The following pieces can now be attempted. REMEMBER to use rest strokes and use the fingering shown.

The numbers by the notes indicate which left hand finger is to be used to hold down the string. Where an "0" appears the note is to played on an open string.

Always use the tips of your left hand fingers to hold down the strings. This helps to avoid the finger pads from touching adjacent strings and thus preventing them from sounding clearly.

For reference the notes as they appear on the music stave, clef (or staff) and the strings used to produce those notes are shown in separate diagrams. Please study these if you have difficulty in recognising particular notes.

Adopt the habit of always looking through the music before attempting to play it.

Note the **KEY SIGNATURE**, the **TIME SIGNATURE** and any additional accidentals within the score.

If there are eighth notes (quavers) in the piece, count the time in eighth notes – one and two and three and etc. This will help you get the timing right.

e.g.

♩.

You will notice that in "Morning has Broken" and "Londonderry Air" that several notes have a dot after them.

NEW RULE.

A DOT AFTER A NOTE LENGTHENS THAT NOTE BY HALF AS MUCH AGAIN.

Therefore a half note (minim) is equal to two quarter notes. 𝅗𝅥 = ♩ ♩

A dotted half note is equal to three quarter notes. 𝅗𝅥. = ♩ ♩ ♩

This means that in bars two and three of "Morning has Broken" for instance, the dotted half note must last for the whole bar i.e. three beats.

In the last two bars of "Morning has Broken" you will see two dotted half notes joined together by a curve.

This indicates that these two notes are joined together and sound as one note lasting six beats, or to put it another way, one note the duration of which is two bars.

MORNING HAS BROKEN

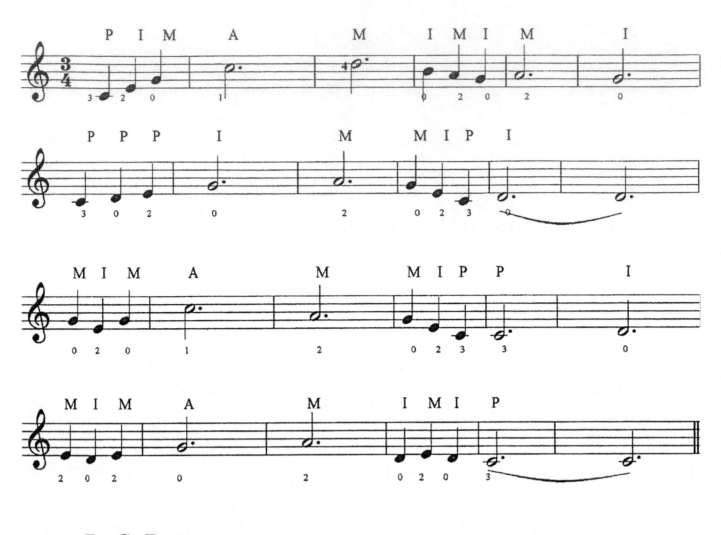

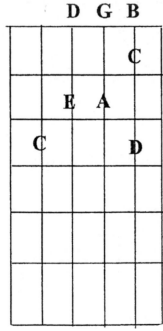

OPEN STRINGS

C D E F G A B C D E

Remember that the letters written above the stave refer to the right hand fingers and the numbers by the notes refer to the left hand fingers.

COCKLES AND MUSSELS

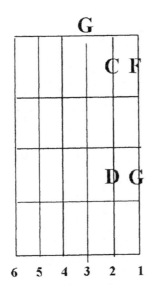

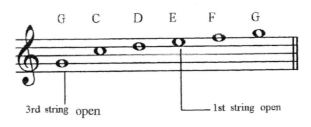

Played on open strings

LONDONDERRY AIR

OPEN STRINGS

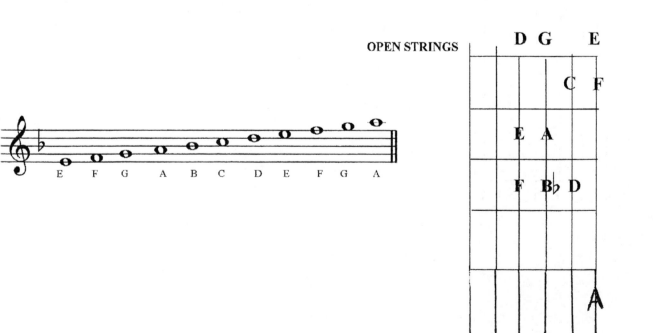

E F G A B C D E F G A

MY GRANDFATHER'S CLOCK

HAPPY BIRTHDAY TO YOU

Use rest strokes

THREE BLIND MICE

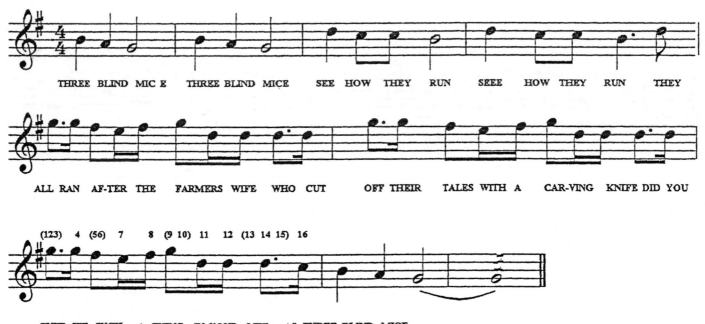

THREE BLIND MIC E   THREE BLIND MICE   SEE HOW THEY RUN   SEEE HOW THEY RUN   THEY

ALL RAN AF-TER THE   FARMERS WIFE   WHO CUT   OFF THEIR   TALES WITH A   CAR-VING KNIFE DID YOU

EVER SEE SUCH   A THING IN YOUR LIFE   AS THREE BLIND MICE

The timing for "Three Blind Mice" is difficult because there are lots of dotted notes. As most of the bars contain semiquavers you will have to count each beat (four crotchets to the bar therefore four beats) in semiquavers.

As shown above the third bar from the end of the piece.

ESPANÕL

Major Scales

There are many reasons why we should learn and practice scales:

1. To ensure that left hand fingers are on their tips.
2. To ensure that left hand fingers are right behind the fret wires and not on them or too far to the left.
3. To create fluency between both hands.
4. To develop flexibility between right hand fingers i, m, i, a, m, a etc with the use of rest strokes.
5. To obtain clear appreciation of rhythm.

In the scales below, the numbers by the notes denote the left hand fingering and the numbers in the circles denote the string on which the notes are to be played.

e.g. ⑥————⌐ means that all notes within the bracket must be played on the sixth string.

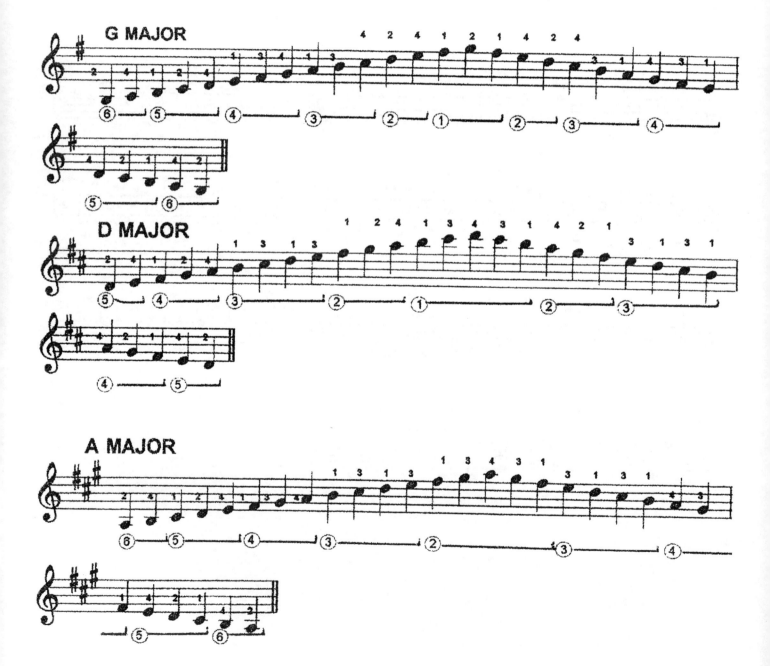

Arpeggios

Arpeggios are formed by playing the notes of a chord separately or in progression. We have already experienced arpeggios in the earlier exercises when we practised chords.

Although the following exercises are written in $^4/_4$ (four crotchets or quarter notes) in the bar notice that the notes are grouped together in threes and that there seems to be more quavers (eight notes) than there should be.

This form of grouping is known as TRIPLETS.

Triplets are a group of three notes played in the time normally taken to play two and are usually indicated by a figure three and a curve placed above or below the group.

With a time signature of $^4/_4$ we would normally expect to find eight eighth notes (quavers) in a bar but when the eighth notes are to be played as triplets there are twelve.

When playing triplets count in threes.

Do you remember the E minor chord? Play it a few times and note how different it sounds to the E major sound.

The minor key gives this study a plaintive sound rather than the full romantic sound of the major.

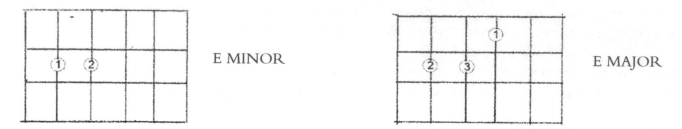

E MINOR   E MAJOR

STUDY IN E MINOR

Now try this piece written in triplets.

Not the inclusion of accidentals – the sharpened G.

When an accidental is added within a bar it applies to all notes with the same letter name until the end of that bar

Notes as they are found on the guitar strings

Notes as they appear on the music staff (stave).

JESU JOY OF MAN'S DESIRING

The following piece of music is a duet.

If you do not have a friend to play with you, learn the top line and then record it on tape or CD. Then learn the second part and play along with your recording.

Do this with both parts.

1.   This is a useful exercise, which will develop:

2.   Your sense of timing.

3.   Your awareness of the different voices within the music.

4.   Your ability to count the timing of a piece and to maintain an even tempo throughout the piece.

Be aware of the accidentals (sharps and flats) in this piece. Remember that a sharp raises a note by a semitone and a flat lowers a note by a semitone.

MELODY FOR TWO

Now is the time to introduce notes, which accompany the melody.

We have already learnt "Cockles and Mussels" as a single note melody. If you look closely at this piece, as given on the next page, you will see that we have introduced what is known as a **BASE LINE** or second melody which uses, in the main, dotted minims.

A dot after a note has the effect of lengthening that note by half its original value. Therefore, in "Cockles and Mussels" the dotted minim is equal to three crotchets and because the piece is written in ¾ time lasts for the whole bars length.

We are now beginning to consider two lines of music. The two lines should be played with equal attention. Listen to the musical impact the bottom line makes on the upper one – the melody.

If we look at the second bar of this version of "Cockles and Mussels" we will see that the lower note (middle C) is encountered on the first beat of the bar and should therefore be played at the same time as the first note of the upper melody.

To play the notes of the bottom melody use the thumb (p).

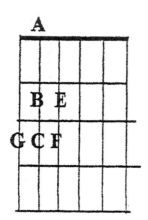

NEW NOTES

COCKLES AND MUSSELS

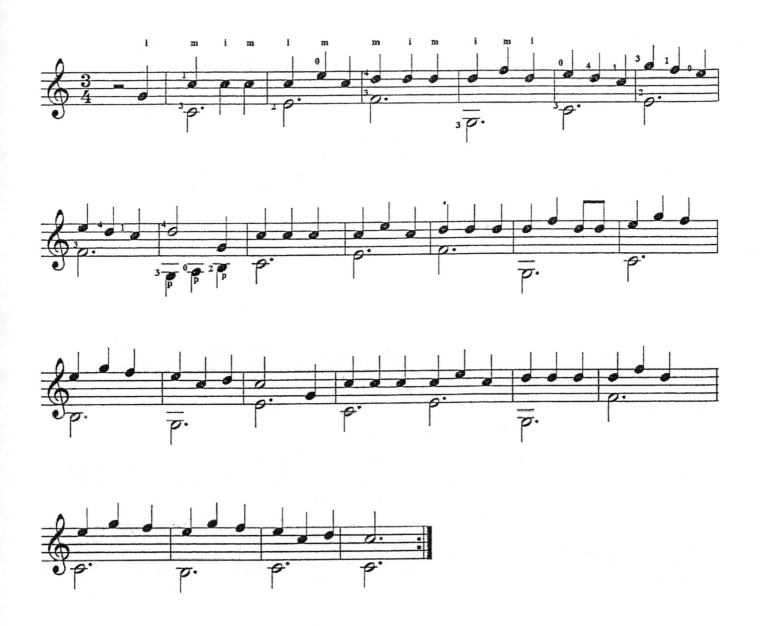

SPRING

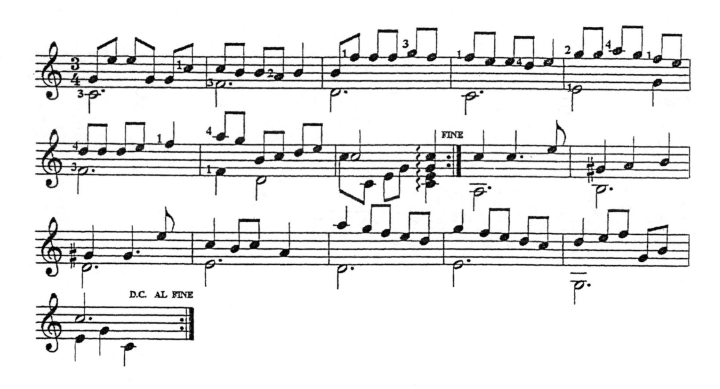

In "Spring" remember that the G in bars ten and eleven is sharpened.

At the end of bar eight the :‖ sign means that you should repeat from the beginning going right through to the end of the piece where another repeat sign appears in addition to the letters "D.C.AL Fine". This means go back to the beginning and play through to the word Fine at bar eight.

The wavy line by the chord at the end of bar eight means that the chord should be played in broken fashion i.e. one note after the other.

MYSTIC PLACES

The following piece incorporates the use of **RESTS**. For every note there is an equivalent rest and illustrations of these can be seen on page 13.

Rests appear where no note or notes are to be played – where silence is required – this can be a very useful and effective tool, as can be seen in the following piece. To achieve this, stop the string from sounding by touching it with a right hand or left hand finger.

In bar two note the four quaver (eighth note) rests in both the top and the bottom melody.

To achieve the required effect play the first chord with p i m a whilst counting (one and two and three and four and).

On the and place p i m a back on the strings but do not pluck them until the next chord is required.

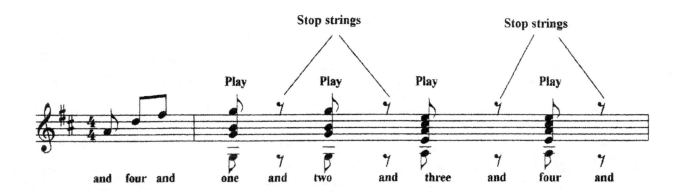

Note that in bars five, seven, eleven and twenty-two half note (minim) and quarter notes (crotchet) rests are used.

Notice that the piece does not start on the first beat of the bar.
A piece of music often starts this way with the missing beats added at the end.

The small note above the first bar tells us at what speed the piece is to be played.

♩ = 106 tell us that one minute must contain 106 quarter notes (crotchets).

Ritardando means getting gradually slower.

SHORT RESTS

Ritardando

SUNSHINE

Minor Scales

For each major scale there is a relative minor scale and the tonic of the minor scale (sometimes known as the root or keynote) is the sixth note of the major scale.

e.g. Scale of C major   C D E F G A B C
                                        :
                                        :   sixth note

The relative minor therefore of C major is A minor.

e.g. Scale of A major (three sharps F C and G)   G A B C (sharp) D E F (sharp) G (sharp)
                                                                          :
                                                                          :   sixth note

The relative minor of G major is therefore F sharp minor.

Comparison of major and minor scales shows us quite clearly the difference between them:-

C Major

A Minor

The third note of the minor scale is different. It is the third note which really decides whether the scale is major or minor. The seventh or leading note is also sharpened producing a big step from F natural to G sharp. The scale with this big step from the sixth to the seventh note is called the Harmonic minor.

There is an alternative way of writing a minor scale known as the melodic minor scale:-

This form of the scale is easier on the ear and is different in that the sixth as well as the seventh note is sharpened ascending. They are lowered by one semitone (see the natural signs) however, when descending.

Now try these minor scales and listen as you play them to the different tonal progression of the melodic and Harmonic minor and compare both with the sound of the major scale.

Minor keys are often used for Folk music because of their somewhat plaintive sound.

Intervals

An interval in music is the distance in pitch between notes.

Intervals are named according to the number of letter names from the lower note to the upper note, both of which are included.

When the two notes of an interval can be found in the same key, the interval is **DIATONIC**. Intervals are known as **MAJOR, MINOR** and **PERFECT**.

Diatonic intervals of C major

Diatonic intervals of A minor

Now here are some more chord shapes for you to try. Use the same practice procedure as before.

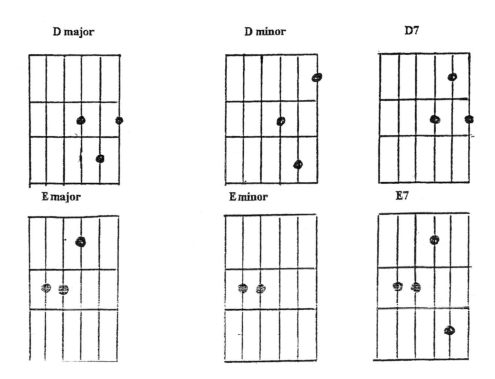

BARRE CHORDS

There are two ways of holding down a barre chord – by using a half barre or a full barre. The requirements of the music will determine which of them is used.

To get an idea of what a barre chord is, imagine the first finger of your left hand as a straight piece of metal placed across some or all of the strings at a particular fret, as per the following illustration.

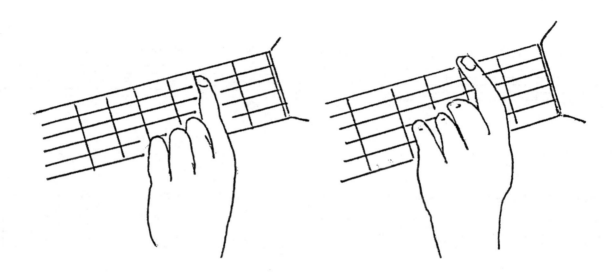

Whenever the barre is applied to five or less strings it is known as a half barre – half in this instance does not always mean three strings only but can mean four or five depending upon the musical requirement.

There is a danger when attempting to hold down a barre chord of applying too much pressure, which has the effect of restricting the movement of the fingers and preventing the production of clear notes.

In order to assess the amount of pressure needed on the barre finger (first finger) hold it lightly against the fifth fret and commence to strum the strings. Slowly increase the pressure until the strings sound clearly. When applying pressure it will help if the finger is rolled slightly towards the fret wire.

Ensure that the fingertip does not project more than necessary beyond the fingerboard and that the creases at the finger joints do not coincide with the strings.

There are several ways of indicating a barre :

B5   BV   C5   Capitasto 5   All indicate a barre at the fifth position

½B5   ½BV   ½C5   All indicate a half barre at the fifth position

NOTE: The barre sign is sometimes used to indicate position only and does not always indicate that a barre or half barre is required.

Arpeggio/barre exercise – Chromatic scale.

A chromatic scale is one that moves in semitones (one fret at a time) and this exercise illustrates this scale nicely.

1. Hold down a full barre at the fifth position with the first finger of the left hand and, using alternating A and M right hand fingers, proceed as follows:

2. Play the first string at the fifth position sixth, seventh and eighth using fingers (left hand) one (holding down the barre) two, three and four.

3. Continue holding down the barre at the fifth position and repeat the exercise on strings five, four, three, two and one.

4. Repeat the entire exercise on the fourth, third, second and first fret.

Always remember when playing barre chords that the minimum amount of pressure should be used to hold down the barre.

Too much pressure on the barre finger will result in the middle joint being forced away from the fretboard resulting in the production of muffled sound.

Remember that the first finger should be as close to the fret wire as possible.
Try rolling the finger slightly towards the fret wire to gain clarity of tone.

The following chords are to be played with a full barre:

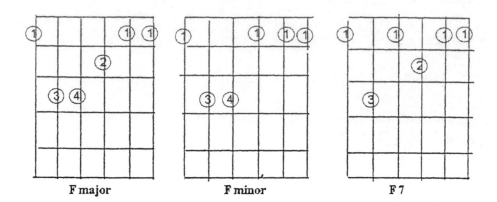

If you find it difficult to hold down a full barre at the first position, hold down the same chord at the fifth position (fret) and strum the strings four times then slide down to the third position and repeat.

Now play the same chord shape in fourth then second then third and finally first position.

To progress further repeat as before but change the chord shape each time:

F major shape   at fifth position
F minor shape   at third position
F7 shape   at fourth position
F major shape   at second position
F minor shape   at third position
F7 shape   at first position

Remember that this is an exercise only and that the true position for these chords is as the chord boxes shown above.

Notes on fifth fret.

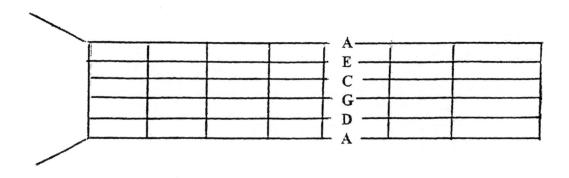

The following notes have all been played before and should now be known.

Play them now with a barre at the fifth position (fifth fret).

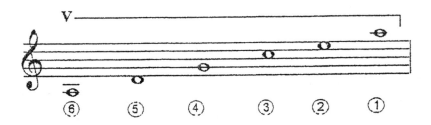

In fact most of the notes found in first position can be found higher up the fretboard. For interest's sake hold down the first string at the first fret(F) and pluck the string. Now count five frets up and play the second string in that position, then count another five frets up and play the third string at that position. Not only are the notes produced all F but they are the same F although slightly different in texture.

Try this exercise as an aid to mastering the Barre chord.

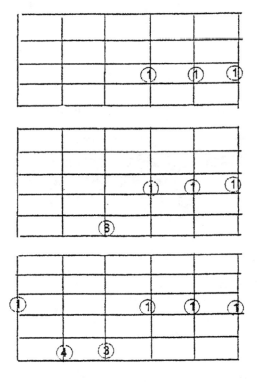

A) Hold down a half barre at the third position and play strings one, two and three only

B) Hold down a half barre as in A but include the fourth string at the fifth position.

C) Hold down the completed barre with strings four and five at the fifth position and play all six strings.

REMEMBER TO TAKE YOUR LEFT HAND AWAY FROM THE GUITAR
AT THE FIRST SIGN OF UNDUE STRAIN.

Barre Exercises

Exercise one rest stroke
Exercise two and three free stroke
Pay in all positions up to ninth

Here is an exercise to improve your mastery of barre chords.

Do not overstrain the muscles between your left hand thumb and forefinger. As soon as you feel strain stop and play something less demanding.

TANGO EL BARRE

An introduction to arpeggios was given on page 27 when we studied the triplets. Now is the time to introduce exercises in specific keys.

ARPEGGIOS

The left hand fingering in the above arpeggios is optional and any good practical fingering is acceptable.

Play with free strokes.

SUMMER JOY

Harmonics

These are exciting sounds, created by touching the strings lightly and lifting the left hand immediately as they are plucked thus causing the strings to vibrate in several sections of its length rather than as one sound. There are two forms to consider. Natural harmonics and Octave harmonics.

Natural harmonics
Twelfth fret

There are several ways of indicating a harmonic note, the most popular being the diamond shape as shown above.

The strongest open harmonics are found at the fifth, seventh and twelfth frets. The above examples are at the twelfth fret.

They can be played in two ways:

1.   With a combination of left and right hand fingers.
2.   With the right hand only using (i) and (m), also used with octave harmonics.

With the tip of the left hand finger lightly touch the first string at the twelfth fret, pluck the string with (a) and immediately lift the left hand finger. The result should be a bell-like note an octave higher. Repeat on the other strings using m.i.p.p.p. Pluck the strings closer to the bridge.

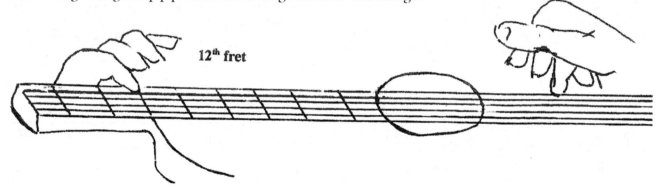

To play with the right hand only place (i) lightly on the string directly over the twelfth fret and pluck the string with (a), immediately release (i). This method is also used to create Octave Harmonics.

Octave Harmonics on first string

Pluck the string directly over the thirteenth fret to produce the F,
fifteenth fret for the G (twelve frets above the left hand position) and so on.

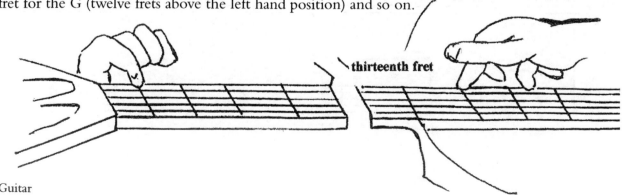

AUTUMN MIST

Sight Reading

One of the greatest joys for a musician is to pick up a piece of music and, after a few minutes' observation, play it.

The following exercises will help you do just that. Follow the following rules. Do not commit them to memory.

1. Look at the time signature and decide how you are going to count the beats in the bar.
2. Look at the key signature and remember which notes if any are to be sharpened or flattened.
3. Are any notes sharpened or flattened apart from those in the key signature and is therefore the music in a major or a minor key?
4. Count a full bar before you start to play and DO NOT STOP until the end of the exercise.

Did you play any of the notes on open strings? Try this exercise again, this time use stopped strings only.

Did you notice the G sharp? Is exercise two in a major or minor key? Play both the above exercises and listen to the difference in tone.

Did you notice the two sharps in the key signature? What key is this exercise in?

The following exercises are a little more difficult and require careful preparation but no longer than thirty seconds.

Did you notice the staccato notes? What does Marziale mean?

ROMANCE

ANONYMOUS

Snaps and Hammers

(Ligado – from the Spanish word *Ligar* – to bind). Also known as a slur.

Snaps and hammers are used to assist in the playing of fast passages by making it possible to produce notes with both hands. Always use the tip of the fingers and be aware of the quality of the note you are producing.

Exercise for ascending Ligado (Hammer).

1. Starting on the fourth string place the first finger of the left hand on the string at the ninth fret. Pluck the string with A of the right hand and "hammer down" on the fourth string at the eleventh fret with the third finger to sound the legado.

2. Place the second finger on the fourth string at the tenth fret, keeping the first finger in position, and pluck the string with M. Hammer down on the fourth tring at the eleventh fret with the fourth finger.

3. After repeating the exercise twice move the first finger down to the eighth fret and repeat the exercise. Carry on in this way down the fret board.

4. Repeat the exercise on the third, second and first strings.

Exercise for descending ligados (Snaps)

To perform this ligado pull the finger down between the strings slightly to the left coming to rest on the lower string.

1. Starting on the fourth string, place the first finger of the left hand on the string at the ninth fret and the third finger on the string at the eleventh fret. Pluck the string with A and "pull off" the third finger to sound the ligado.

2. Place the second finger on the left hand on the fourth string at the tenth fret and the fourth finger on the string at the twelfth fret. Pluck the string with M and "pull off" the fourth finger to sound the ligado.

3. Repeat the exercise twice then move the first finger down to the eighth fret and repeat the exercise.

LIGADO STUDIES

LIGADO MOMENTS

LIGADO FROLICS

SEMPRE A'MORE – LA – CHITARRA

Dedicated to Nemanja Bogunovic

I have not included any performance directions in the previous pages, principally because I wanted you to develop your own "musicality". From this moment forward, however, you will be learning music that includes the specific requirements of the composer with regard to speed, volume and expression.

It is therefore important to learn some of the most common performance instructions.

All the following are Italian, all of which would be required learning were you to be considering the Royal Associated Board practical exams grade one and two.

Accelerando (or accel) –	getting gradually quicker
Adagio –	slow
Allegretto –	fairly quick (but not as quick as allegro)
Allegro –	quick (literally "cheerful")
Andante –	at a medium "walking" pace
Cantabile –	in a singing style
Crescendo –	gradually getting louder
Da capo (or D.C.) –	repeat from the beginning
Dal Segno (or D.S.) –	repeat from the sign s/s
Decrescendo (or decresc) –	gradually getting quieter
Dimunuendo (or dim.) –	gradually getting quieter
Fine –	the end
f (= forte) –	loud
ff (= fortissimo) –	very loud
Legato –	smoothly
Lento –	slow
Mezzo –	half
Grave –	very slow, solemn
Graxioso –	graceful

Larghetto –	rather slow (but not as slow as largo)
Largo –	slow, stately
Ma –	but
Maestoso –	majestic
Mano –	less
Molto –	very, much
Mosso, moto –	movement (meno mosso: slower; Con moto: with motion)
Non –	not
Piu –	more
Presto –	fast (faster than allegro)
Senza –	without
Sf, sfz (= sforzando or sforzato) –	forced, accented
Simile –	in a similar way
Sostenuto –	sustained
Tenuto –	held
Troppo –	too much (non troppo: not too much)
Vivace, vivo –	lively, quick

Now that you have completed the studies within this tutor you should have a good basis in technique and musical knowledge to take you further in your enjoyment of the guitar and its sound.

The music contained herein should give you a basis repertoire from which to expand. Do not be a student all the while. Play pieces from your memory and enjoy listening to the sounds you make. Enjoy the praise from your family and friends when they like what they hear.

YOU DESERVE IT!

> Finally, on the subject of practise, I would like to share with you a method taken from the "readers' letters" page of the *Times* newspaper written by a music teacher.
>
> "When my colleagues and I questioned employers of our graduates, several stated that they rated highly the methods used in practising an instrument or voice.
>
> Students learn to identify a problem; isolate it; apply or invent an exercise to overcome it; work at it; replace it in its context; then move on to the next problem – a sequential process as valuable outside of music as within."
>
> George Pratt. Emeretius Proffessor of Music at the University of Huddersfield.

One more quotation for you, from Shakespeare:

> "If music be the food of love PLAY ON."

The following pieces have been written by me as an encouragement to practice.

All of them bring back a special memory of students as far away as the Arizona desert in America.

Making music is one of my few pastimes which does not require being better than or beating anyone else. As a hobby there is no "must" about practising though the more we try the better we become. Playing the guitar is supposed to be fun, relaxing and pleasurable.

If you have the talent to play for other people you have the satisfaction of witnessing their pleasure as a result of your efforts.

There is no better sense of fulfilment than seeing the appreciation on people's faces after a piece of music played well.

I hope that by producing this tutor I have put a smile on *your* face.

When the world's pressures create anxiety and stress in your mind, pick up your guitar and play for a while. Engross yourself in the joy of music – the joy of your guitar

VLUNNOM SIYANIE

Transcribed for guitar by John Snowdon on behalf of Olga Stone

Introduction

Theme

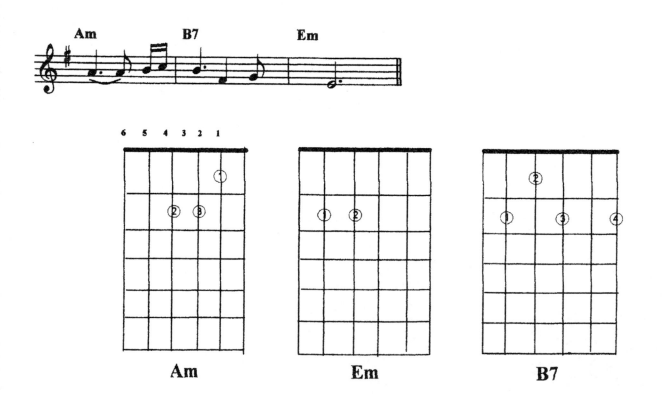

EULOGY for SAL

EXERCISE FOR SHEA

Remember to count a bar before you start playing "one and two and three and four and..."

②   This means play all the notes within this perenthisis on the second string.

⌢   This means pause before continuing and sustain the note (notes).

4 ⟍   This means play all these notes with the fourth left hand finger.

The key signature of this exercise has one flat but there are several "accidentals" within the music to consider.

Remember that an accidental introduced to a note is sustained for all notes of the same name for one bar only. E.g. the C sharp in the last bar second beat also applies to the C in the last chord (third and fourth beats).

AMBER'S ELEVEN

HAPPY BIRTHDAY TO YOU
ALEXANDRA

Arranged by John Snowdon

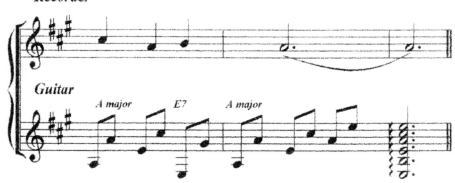

JILL'S DAY

Meditation

NEW PATHWAYS

AMBER-LING BLUES

AMBER'S TWELVE (Beats to the Bar)

LIFE BEGINS AT FORTY

GARRYANNA

A celebration of the wedding between Anna Snowdon and Garry Walker

Composed by John Snowdon

EMMI-EL-HAMM

معاً الى الأبد فى حبّ بدون نهاية

John Snowdon
(Granpa John)

REFLECTION

 = 65

With Feeling

H XII

H V ⑤

ABOVE THE SEVENTH

Lightning Source UK Ltd.
Milton Keynes UK
UKOW01f0124250814

237443UK00005B/83/P